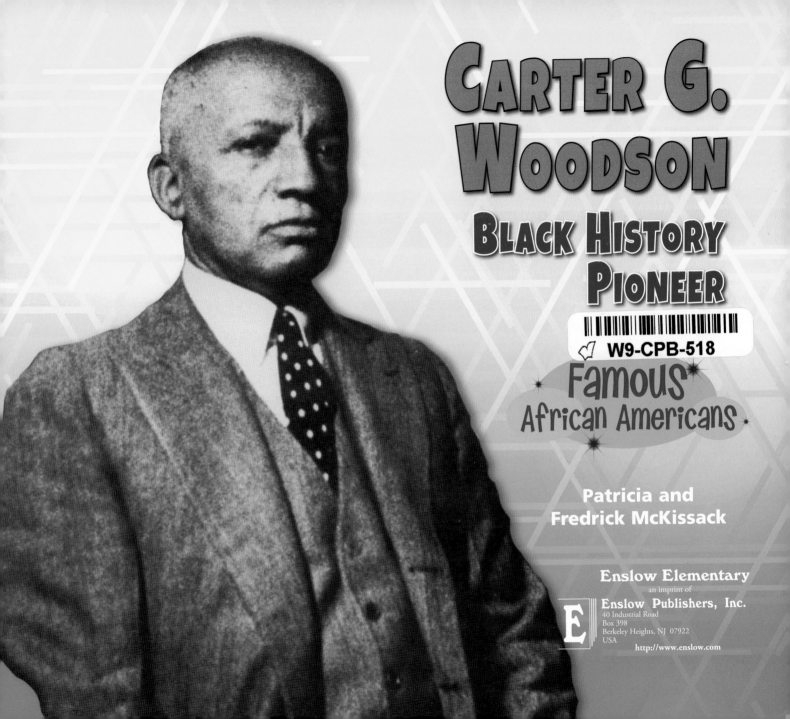

CARTER G. WOODSON

BLACK HISTORY PIONEER

W9-CPB-518

Famous African Americans

Patricia and Fredrick McKissack

Enslow Elementary
an imprint of
Enslow Publishers, Inc.
40 Industrial Road
Box 398
Berkeley Heights, NJ 07922
USA
http://www.enslow.com

To Barbara, T.J., and C.C.

Enslow Elementary, an imprint of Enslow Publishers, Inc.

Enslow Elementary® is a registered trademark of Enslow Publishers, Inc.

Revised edition of *Carter G. Woodson: The Father of Black History* © 1991

Library of Congress Cataloging-in-Publication Data

McKissack, Pat, 1944-
Carter G. Woodson : Black history pioneer / Patricia and Fredrick McKissack.
    p. cm. — (Famous African Americans)
Previously published: Carter G. Woodson. Berkeley Heights, NJ : Enslow Publishers, ©2002
Summary: "A simple biography for early readers about Carter G. Woodson's life"—Provided by publisher.
Includes bibliographical references and index.
ISBN 978-0-7660-4109-7
1. Woodson, Carter Godwin, 1875-1950—Juvenile literature. 2. African American historians—Biography—Juvenile literature. 3. Historians—United States—Biography—Juvenile literature. 4. African Americans—Historiography—Juvenile literature. I. McKissack, Fredrick. II. Title.
  E175.5.W65M35 2013
  973'.049607307202—dc23
  [B]

            2012024624

Future editions:
Paperback ISBN 978-1-4644-0195-4
ePUB ISBN 978-1-4645-1108-0
PDF ISBN 978-1-4646-1108-7

Printed in the United States of America

082012 Lake Book Manufacturing, Inc., Melrose Park, IL

10 9 8 7 6 5 4 3 2 1

To Our Readers: We have done our best to make sure all Internet Addresses in this book were active and appropriate when we went to press. However, the author and the publisher have no control over and assume no liability for the material available on those Internet sites or on other Web sites they may link to. Any comments or suggestions can be sent by e-mail to comments@enslow.com or to the address on the back cover.

Every effort has been made to locate all copyright holders of material used in this book. If any errors or omissions have occurred, corrections will be made in future editions of this book.

♻ Enslow Publishers, Inc., is committed to printing our books on recycled paper. The paper in every book contains 10% to 30% post-consumer waste (PCW). The cover board on the outside of each book contains 100% PCW. Our goal is to do our part to help young people and the environment too!

Photo Credits: Library of Congress, Prints & Photographs Division, p. 13; Moorland-Spingarn Research Center, Howard University, pp. 4, 16; National Archives, pp. 1, 3, 20.

Illustration Credits: Ned O., pp. 7, 8, 10, 14.

Cover Photo: National Archives

Words in bold type are are explained in Words to Know on page 22.

Series Consultant:
Russell Adams, PhD
Emeritus Professor
Afro-American Studies
Howard University

CONTENTS

Carter Woodson's parents were slaves. He spent much of his life teaching others about black history.

CHAPTER 1
FAMILY STORIES

• •

The first history lessons Carter Woodson learned were about his own family. His mother, Anne Eliza Riddle, was born a **slave**. She told stories about her life.

Carter's father told him stories, too. James Henry Woodson was also born a slave. His **master** beat him all the time.

One day James took the whip away from his master and beat him with it. A group of men came to kill James. But he ran and hid in the woods for many, many days.

It was near the end of the **Civil War**. Soldiers from the North were in Virginia. They found James in the woods. They told him he was free. James soon joined the **Union Army**.

The war ended in April 1865. Soon after, James and Anne met and married. They moved to Huntington, West Virginia.

In 1874 they moved back to New Canton, Virginia. They bought a small farm. Carter Godwin Woodson was born there on December 19, 1875.

When the Union soldiers found Carter's father, they told him that he would no longer be a slave. He was free!

Carter learned how to read even though he could not go to school very often.

CHAPTER 2
NEVER TOO LATE TO LEARN

· ·

Carter's father couldn't read or write. But he always told his seven children, "It is never too late to learn."

Carter had to help out on the family farm. There wasn't much time for school. Still he learned how to read. He read every day.

When Carter was sixteen years old, he went to West Virginia with his older brothers. There he worked on the railroad and in a **coal mine**.

By 1893, Anne and James had moved back to Huntington, West Virginia. Carter had two younger sisters. They wanted to go to Douglass High School. Carter wanted to go there, too.

But he was eighteen years old. "It is never too late to learn," he told the **principal**.

As a high school principal, Carter taught his students the importance of reading and learning.

Carter had learned a lot on his own. He did very well on a test. So they let Carter start at Douglass High School. Then he surprised everyone when he **graduated** eighteen months later.

Next Carter went to **college**. After a few months, he was asked to be the principal of a school. He had that job for two years. In the summers, he went to school.

In 1900, Carter was asked to be the principal of Douglass High School back in Huntington. He was proud to take the job. He stayed there three years.

Carter read every day. He tried to learn something new every day. He read to his students. And he always told them, "It is never too late to learn."

CHAPTER 3
"SHAKE THE LOMBOY TREE"

In August 31, 1903, a letter came for Carter. He had been asked to come teach in the **Philippine Islands.** His work began on December 19, 1903.

Something was wrong. The children weren't learning. They didn't like to read. The other teachers said the children were lazy. Or their mothers and fathers didn't care. Carter wouldn't stop trying.

One day he sang a song for his students: "Come Shake the Apple Tree." But apples don't grow in the Philippines! So Carter changed the words to "Come Shake the **Lomboy** Tree." A lomboy is a kind of plum. The children loved the song. They wanted to learn it. And they did.

In the Philippines, Carter taught children like those shown here. The hut behind them is their classroom.

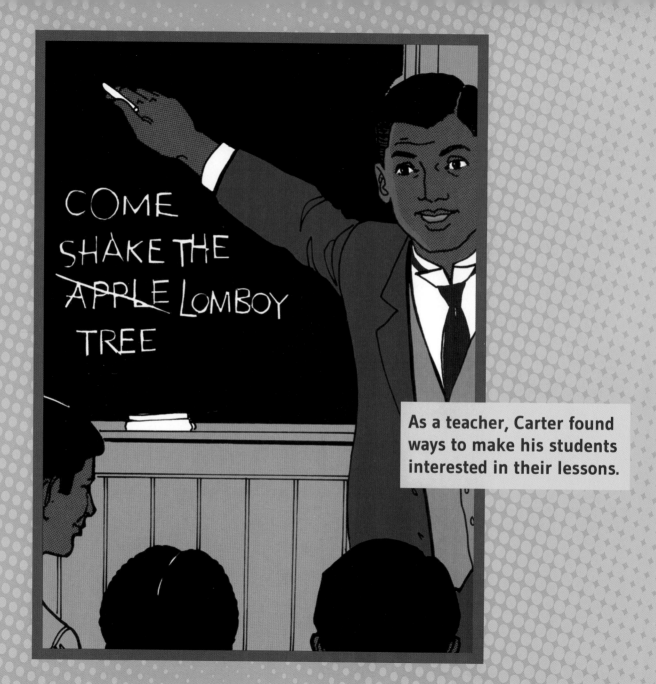

As a teacher, Carter found ways to make his students interested in their lessons.

Carter learned Spanish. He taught the children about their own history and **heroes**. The children were proud of who they were. Soon they were reading and learning quickly.

After that, Carter put away the books. They were written for American children.

Carter thought about the school books back home. They didn't have much black history in them. Carter wrote home. "It is time to 'Come Shake the Lomboy Tree' in American schools."

Carter Woodson liked to look his best. He never married.

CHAPTER 4
TEACH OURSELVES

Each summer Carter came home. He studied history at the University of Chicago. He came home for good in 1908. He needed to learn more. So he went to the University of Chicago. He graduated in March. He continued his studies and earned a higher **degree** in August of that same year.

Then Woodson went to Harvard University in Massachusetts. There he worked on the highest degree a student can earn—a **Ph.D**. He received his Ph.D. in history in 1912. With that degree, he was called Dr. Woodson.

Dr. Woodson took a job at M Street High School in **Washington, D.C.** There he taught history, French, and Spanish.

History books still didn't have much about black people in them. "We must teach ourselves," he said. At his school, black history was taught.

In 1914, Dr. Woodson became a member of the **American Negro Academy**. The group found and saved African-American writings. They wanted to show that black people had done many important things in history.

Dr. Woodson started the **Association for the Study of Negro Life and History** in 1915. "We will teach ourselves about ourselves," he said.

CHAPTER 5
BE PROUD

Most schoolchildren didn't know about the important things black people had done. Dr. Woodson wrote about these great African Americans.

Dr. Woodson had an idea that would help people learn more about black history.

Two of Dr. Woodson's heroes were Frederick Douglass and Abraham Lincoln. Douglass fought against slavery. And President Lincoln freed the slaves. Both men were born in February.

In February 1926, Dr. Woodson planned the first "Negro History Week" program. It was the start of what is now called Black History Month.

Dr. Woodson studied and wrote about **Africa**, too. He wanted black people to know about their African **ancestors**.

Dr. Woodson wrote many books. He also started a magazine about African-American history.

"Africa has a great past," he told schoolchildren all over the country. "Be proud!"

Dr. Woodson stopped teaching to run the association full-time. He never married. He lived over the association's office in a small apartment. He was a neat man who liked nice clothes. He was always busy, but he was hardly ever late.

On April 3, 1950, Dr. Woodson was late for work. Something had to be wrong. And it was. He had died during the night.

Dr. Woodson's work helped show the world that African Americans had much to be proud of. Today his work goes on.

WORDS TO KNOW

Africa—The second largest continent in the world.

American Negro Academy—An organization that found and saved African-American writings.

ancestors—People who lived long ago, and are related by family or race.

Association for the Study of Negro Life and History—An organization started to teach black people about themselves and their history.

Civil War—A war fought within one country. The United States Civil War was fought between northern and southern states from 1861 to 1865.

coal mine—A mine is a place in the ground where minerals like coal, gold, and silver are dug out.

college—A school beyond high school.

degree—A signed piece of paper that a college or university gives a person when he or she has graduated.

graduate—To finish all the studies at a school.

hero—A person who is looked up to because of the things he or she does.

lomboy tree—A plum tree that grows in the Philippine Islands.

master—A ruler or a person who controls another. Someone who owns a slave is called a master.

National Association for the Advancement of Colored People (NAACP)—An organization started to help all Americans gain equal rights and protection under the law.

Ph.D.—The highest degree a student can earn from a university. It means doctor of philosophy.

Philippine Islands—A group of small islands in the South Pacific Ocean.

principal—The head of a school.

slave—A person who is owned by another. That person can be bought or sold.

Union Army—The army that fought for the North in the Civil War.

Washington, D.C.—The place where the United States government is located. (D.C. stands for District of Columbia.)

LEARN MORE

BOOKS

Haskins, Jim. *Carter G. Woodson: The Man Who Put "Black" in American History.* Brookfield, Conn.: Millbrook Press, 2000.

Kamma, Anne. *If You Lived When There Was Slavery in America.* New York: Scholastic, 2006.

Sanders, Nancy I. *A Kid's Guide to African American History.* Chicago: Chicago Review Press, 2007.

WEB SITES

Carter G. Woodson National Historic Site
<http://www.nps.gov/cawo/>

Dr. Carter G. Woodson African American Museum
<http://www.woodsonmuseum.org>

INDEX